Author: Isaac Ravenscroft

ISBN HARDBACK: 978-9916-90-816-7

ISBN PAPERBACK: 978-9916-90-817-4

Secrets in the Stillness

Whispers dance on a breath of night,
Flickering shadows embrace the light.
In the heart of silence, truths unfold,
Ancient stories in the stillness told.

Beneath the moon's soft, watchful gaze,
Secrets linger in a tranquil haze.
Each rustling leaf, a story shared,
In the stillness, the soul is bared.

Echoes of dreams drift through the air,
Carrying wishes, fragile and rare.
In tender moments, lives entwined,
A tapestry woven, fate defined.

Listen closely to the soft refrain,
In the quiet, love hides its pain.
From the depths of calm, a stir reveals,
Secrets kept in the stillness, heals.

Discord of the Unheard

Lost in chaos, where silence reigns,
Voices tremble in forgotten chains.
Echoes wander, seeking a sound,
In the discord, truths are drowned.

Words unspoken build a heavy wall,
In the shadows, we ache and fall.
Broken rhythms pulse beneath the skin,
In the chaos, we search within.

The heart beats loud, yet remains unheard,
A symphony lost, a muted bird.
In the stillness, a longing cry,
In the discord, dreams fade and die.

Yet within the void, a spark ignites,
From the silence, emerge the fights.
In the struggle, we carve a way,
Finding meaning in the disarray.

Ballad of Broken Silences

Upon the edge of twilight's grace,
Lies the melody of a fading trace.
Each silence shatters like glass on stone,
In the fragments, we find what's grown.

Gentle echoes of laughter past,
Whispered moments that will not last.
In the brokenness, a tale to tell,
A ballad woven in wishing well.

Heartbeats resonate in empty rooms,
Amidst the silence, a blossom blooms.
Faded voices bark at the night,
In their echo, we seek the light.

Through the cracks of sorrow, hope seeps through,
A symphony born from pain anew.
In shattered silences, we sing along,
The ballad of life, forever strong.

Harmony in the Gloom

Amidst the shadows, a gentle hum,
A melody soft, as darkness comes.
In the heart of night, harmony blooms,
Finding beauty within the glooms.

Soft whispers weave through the cold air,
In the silence, all hearts lay bare.
Underneath stars, dreams intertwined,
In the gloom, a solace we find.

The world draped in a velvet shroud,
O'er the silence, a soft mist cloud.
In every sorrow, a thread of grace,
In the darkness, we find our place.

Let the moonlight cradle the night,
In the gloom, we discover our light.
With every note, our spirits rise,
In harmony's arms, darkness lies.

Discordant Breath

In the rustle of the leaves,
Voices clash and intertwine,
Music lost in whispers,
Nature's discord starts to shine.

Echoes dance on fleeting winds,
Sorrow mingles with delight,
A symphony of chaos,
Breaking through the still of night.

Shadows of Composed Solitude

In the corner, silence dwells,
Shadows stretch and softly weave,
Thoughts drift like distant bells,
In solitude, we learn to grieve.

A quiet heart sings gently,
Melodies of what we face,
Each note a soft reminder,
Of time's delicate embrace.

Opus of the Unheard

Whispers caught in fleeting dreams,
Music flows beneath the skin,
Light and dark in tangled seams,
An opus waits where we begin.

Notes unplayed in hidden hearts,
Yearning to find voice aligned,
In the silence, art departs,
Unraveled threads of the blind.

Traces of Lonely Sonatas

A lone pianist at dusk,
Fingers dance on empty keys,
Echoes linger in the husk,
Melancholy in the breeze.

Each sonata whispers low,
Tracing paths of bygone days,
In the quiet, feelings flow,
Carved in time through soft arrays.

The Quiet Between Us

In silence we find our space,
Two souls adrift in gentle grace.
Words are soft, like falling snow,
In the stillness, feelings grow.

Moments linger, breaths align,
Time stands still, a sacred sign.
Eyes meet softly, no need to speak,
In this quiet, love feels sweet.

The world outside fades away,
In your presence, I choose to stay.
Each heartbeat echoes, pure and true,
In the quiet, it's just us two.

Auras of Lingering Shadows

Beneath the moon's soft silver glow,
Whispers dance in shadows low.
Auras flicker, secrets shared,
In the night, our souls laid bare.

Echoes of laughter fill the air,
Haunting memories everywhere.
Lingering glances, touch of hands,
In twilight's embrace, love expands.

Yet shadows draw, a veil of doubt,
But in the dark, we'll work it out.
Through every trial, we find our way,
In the silence, let love stay.

Interwoven Threads of Emotion

Threads of color, rich and bright,
Woven through the fabric of night.
Every heartbeat, a stitch in time,
Creating a tapestry, so sublime.

Pain and joy, they twist and turn,
In the loom of love, we yearn.
Each revelation, a new design,
Together, our lives intertwine.

As shadows fade, light takes its place,
In every moment, a warm embrace.
Interwoven, our spirits soar,
Through every thread, we're evermore.

The Heart's Lullaby

In quiet whispers, night descends,
The heart beats soft, as daylight ends.
Crickets serenade the moon,
With every note, our souls attune.

Dreams take flight in tranquil skies,
Where love's soft lullaby never dies.
With every sigh, the stars align,
In the dark, your heart is mine.

Rest your head, let worries fade,
In gentle arms, love is laid.
The night enfolds us, sweet and slow,
In the heart's lullaby, let love grow.

Gentle Ebb of Hope

In the twilight of day, we sigh,
Waves whisper softly, a lullaby.
Stars awaken, a soothing glow,
Guiding dreams where hopes can grow.

Through shadows we wander, hearts align,
Each step a promise, gentle and fine.
With every heartbeat, faith does rise,
In the stillness, courage flies.

Hints of Nostalgia in Silence

Echoes of laughter dance in the air,
Moments now faded, treasures rare.
Whispers of memories linger nonetheless,
Softly they beckon, emotions confess.

A photograph's touch, a tender embrace,
Time weaves its magic, a wistful trace.
In the silence, stories unfold,
Hints of nostalgia, forever retold.

Breath of the Untold

Veils of the night, secrets entwined,
Silhouettes whisper, shadows aligned.
Beneath the moon's gaze, stories take flight,
Carried on wings, into the night.

The voice of the heart, soft as a sigh,
Reveals the unspoken, beneath the sky.
Every breath shared, a tale to unfold,
Enveloped in silence, the truth is bold.

Ethereal Wind of Forgotten Songs

A breeze stirs gently, through ancient trees,
Carrying melodies, lost like memories.
Each note a whisper, a longing to belong,
The spirit of ages, in a timeless song.

Fluttering pages, of stories old,
In the twilight's hush, their magic unfolds.
Ethereal echoes, drift through the night,
Reminding the heart, of love's pure light.

Sotto Voce Whispers

In twilight's soft embrace, we speak,
Words drenched in the hush of night,
Fingers brush against the world,
Secrets carried in moonlight's flight.

Hearts murmur, shadows blend,
Echoes lost in the stillness,
A dance of thoughts unspun,
In silence, we find our witness.

Rhythms pulse beneath the skin,
Subtle tones of hopes and fears,
In whispered dreams, we begin,
To weave the fabric of our years.

Out in the quiet, where souls sing,
Harmony in each soft breath,
Together we unfurl our wings,
Embracing the depths of our depth.

Echo Chamber of Longing

Words ripple through this hollow space,
Carved by echoes of desire,
In every sigh, a fleeting trace,
A heart ignited, an inner fire.

Reflections dance upon the walls,
Memories of whispers past,
In chambers deep, the silence calls,
Yearning for shadows that last.

With every heartbeat, truth unfolds,
Reverberations of the soul,
A story written, yet untold,
Eclipsing all that once was whole.

Caught in the web of time's embrace,
We wander lost in endless night,
In the echo, we find our place,
Longing shapes the faintest light.

Sighs in Shadowy Corners

In dim-lit rooms where memories hide,
Sighs mingle with the dust and air,
Whispers linger, shadows bide,
Stories woven in the bare.

Each corner holds a silent plea,
Grief and joy in tandem throng,
Faint silhouettes speak softly,
Reciting the verses of a song.

The quiet glimmers of the past,
Haunting notes of love's refrain,
In every sigh, a shadow cast,
In every heart, a trace of pain.

Yet still we linger in these seams,
Embracing all that time has kissed,
For in the sighs, we find our dreams,
Wrapped in the shadows, we exist.

The Intermission of Dreams

Between the beats of hopes and fears,
A pause where quietude prevails,
In gentle moments lost to years,
We sail on dream-etched trails.

The curtain draws, and silence flows,
A theater carved from tender light,
Where each heart's longing gently knows,
That night will cradle us in flight.

In this intermission, souls unite,
A canvas waits for brush and hue,
In dreams we dance, soft and bright,
Sketching the wishes, pure and true.

When dawn returns, we'll take our place,
In the story yet to be,
But for now, we linger in grace,
Embracing dreams, wild and free.

Whispers of Unheard Melodies

In the stillness of the night,
Soft whispers dance through air.
Notes unplayed call to me,
Awakening what's rare.

Breezes carry secrets sweet,
From places far away.
They swirl like phantom dreams,
In the twilight's gentle sway.

Each shadow hums a tune,
Lost in quiet despair.
Yet hope lingers softly,
With melodies to share.

In hushed corners of my soul,
Resounding truth expands.
Whispers of unheard melodies,
Embrace me with their hands.

Echoes of Quiet Longing

Shadows linger in the dusk,
Where memories intertwine.
Each echo speaks of longing,
A heart's silent design.

Moonlight drapes a silver cloak,
Over dreams left behind.
Voices whisper what once was,
Yet love remains enshrined.

Each heartbeat thrums with yearning,
A rhythm soft and slow.
In the silence, truth resounds,
A melody we know.

Tender sighs fill the air,
As stars blink in their flight.
Echoes of quiet longing,
Guide us through the night.

Hushed Harmonies of the Heart

In the cradle of the night,
Harmonies softly weep.
Each note a gentle promise,
That echoes through my sleep.

With every breath, a whisper,
A song of love's embrace.
Silent chords intertwining,
In passion's secret space.

Through the veil of stillness,
I feel your spirit near.
Hushed harmonies of the heart,
A symphony sincere.

In the quiet of the moment,
As shadows start to part,
Melodies bring me closer,
To the depths of my heart.

Soliloquies in the Silence

In the stillness I can hear,
Voices that softly plead.
Soliloquies of the soul,
Where thoughts take flight and lead.

Whispers threaded with the light,
Of dreams that dare to rise.
In the silence, truth is found,
Reflected in the skies.

Lonely echoes paint the night,
With colors calm and bold.
Each phrase a sacred secret,
In stories yet untold.

As shadows weave their tapestry,
My heart begins to sing.
Soliloquies in the silence,
A quiet, cherished thing.

Echoing Emotions in the Quiet

Whispers dance on the gentle breeze,
Memories linger beneath the trees.
A heartbeats' rhythm, soft yet clear,
Echoes of love that draw us near.

Shadows flicker in fading light,
Silent secrets hid from sight.
In quiet spaces, feelings bloom,
Emotions wander, finding room.

Nightfall cradles our unspoken dreams,
Where silence flows like silver streams.
Every glance, a story told,
In the hush, our truths unfold.

Stillness wraps around our souls,
In tender moments, the world consoles.
With every pulse, a silent vow,
In echoes, we find our way somehow.

Overture of Unexpressed Love

Eyes meet like stars within the night,
A symphony plays, hidden from sight.
Words unsaid float in the air,
The heart composes, delicate, rare.

Soft sighs cradle the weight of dreams,
Unseen connections in silent streams.
Each heartbeat resonates with grace,
Love's overture in this sacred space.

Lingering touches, electric and bold,
Tales of affection left untold.
In the shadows, the music grows,
In silence, our passion glows.

Every glance is a note, a tease,
The harmony sways with gentle ease.
In this dance of quiet desire,
Together we build the hidden fire.

Cadence of Sighs at Dusk

Dusk descends, weaving tales of old,
In twilight's grip, our dreams unfold.
The wind carries whispers of the heart,
In every sigh, we play our part.

Shadows lengthen, the day concedes,
Echoes of laughter, the heart's decrees.
With every breath, the evening sighs,
A cadence born under fading skies.

Stars awaken, shy and bright,
Guiding lost souls in the night.
A tapestry woven with softest threads,
In sighs, the language of love spreads.

As night's embrace settles in close,
In every moment, we feel the prose.
Together we stand at dusk's sweet door,
In the silence, we long for more.

Silent Strokes of a Hidden Palette

Colors blend in a world unseen,
Each hue whispers what might have been.
Brushes dance on an empty slate,
Creating worlds we can't relate.

A palette hidden, rich and deep,
Where silent dreams softly creep.
With every stroke, emotions flow,
In colors bright and shadows low.

Silence speaks in vibrant tones,
Crafting beauty where love condones.
In hidden strokes, our stories lie,
An artful glance, a heart's soft sigh.

The canvas breathes with gentle grace,
In quiet corners, we find our place.
With each layer, secrets abound,
In silence, our love can be found.

The Language of Lost Whispers

In shadows deep where silence dwells,
Soft echoes drift like distant bells.
Secrets fade in twilight's kiss,
A world unseen, a ghostly bliss.

Words unspoken, like misty sighs,
Trace the contours of hidden ties.
We speak in dreams, in fleeting light,
The language lost, a whispered flight.

Reverberations of Gentle Hearts

In the quiet pulse of tender days,
A heartbeat whispers, softly sways.
Harmony blooms where love resides,
Reflecting truth in gentle tides.

Each glance a note, each smile a song,
Together we dance, where we belong.
In every breath, our spirits meet,
Reverberations, a rhythm sweet.

Chords of Muffled Wishes

Beneath the stars, desires hum,
A tapestry of dreams to come.
Muffled wishes ride the night,
Seeking solace, seeking light.

In whispered hopes, our spirits soar,
Chords entwined, forevermore.
The hush of night, a canvas bare,
Painting futures in the air.

Rhapsody of Absent Words

In the space where silence breathes,
Absent words, like autumn leaves.
Each thought a melody in the air,
Rhapsody sung in moments rare.

A glance, a sigh, the heart does speak,
In poetry's hush, we find the peak.
The language of souls, a dance so bold,
In rhapsody's weave, our story unfolds.

The Subtle Dance of Emotions

In twilight's gentle grace, we sway,
Feelings flicker, drift, and play.
Hearts entwined in soft embrace,
Whispers linger, time won't stay.

Beneath the stars, our secrets roam,
A silent language, found at home.
Each glance a tale, each touch a thread,
In shadows cast, where words are fed.

We twirl on edges, bold yet shy,
With every heartbeat, we can fly.
An unchained rhythm, light and free,
In this embrace, just you and me.

As night unfolds its velvet veil,
We'll dance through dreams, we'll leave a trail.
In the subtle dance of what we feel,
Our souls in sync, forever real.

Veils of Muffled Melancholy

Underneath the weight of gray,
A soft lament, a silent play.
Shadows whisper, moments fade,
In the stillness, hope is laid.

Glimmers of light through heavy clouds,
Voices lost in muted crowds.
Yearning souls in quiet plight,
Searching for the warmth of light.

Each sigh a testament to pain,
Echos linger like gentle rain.
In the heart where shadows dwell,
Muffled stories weave a spell.

Through the veils, a cautious spark,
Guides us gently through the dark.
With each step, we find our way,
In muffled tones, life finds its say.

Phrases Left Unspoken

In glances shared, our truth remains,
A language lost, yet still contains.
Words unformed, like morning mist,
Silent promises, a fragile tryst.

Between the lines, we breathe our fears,
A world of thoughts, unshed tears.
What could be said hangs in the air,
Echoes of love, suspended, rare.

The weight of all that's left unsaid,
Cradles dreams within our head.
Each moment holds a breath so deep,
In this silence, secrets keep.

Yet still we find a way to speak,
In tender touches, soft and meek.
Though phrases left may haunt and cling,
Our hearts compose a song to sing.

Hushed Interludes of Transition

Between the chapters, time stands still,
Caught in echoes, the world we fill.
Silent spaces where thoughts align,
Softly woven like a sign.

These interludes, where futures breath,
In quiet moments, lies our wreath.
Paths diverge, yet still they meet,
In tender glances, bittersweet.

Each pause, a canvas, vast and bare,
Inviting dreams to linger there.
With every shift, a chance to grow,
A silent dance, the ebb and flow.

As we traverse this winding road,
Through hushed transitions, hearts explode.
In every stillness, there's a spark,
Guiding us softly through the dark.

Whispers of Unshed Tears

In shadows deep where silence waits,
A sigh unfurls, a heart that aches.
The night cradles forgotten dreams,
As starlight weaves through silent streams.

Each drop that falls, a story told,
Of moments lost, of dreams so bold.
The whispered winds, a gentle plea,
From waters blue, to set them free.

With every breath, the stillness stings,
A ghost of hope on fragile wings.
Yet through the haze, a spark will shine,
A glimpse of joy, a thread divine.

So let us weep, for tears will heal,
The scars of time, the wounds we feel.
In whispers soft, the heart can mend,
And find its way, a path to blend.

Evocations in Silence

Amidst the hush, where time stands still,
A quiet thought, a fleeting thrill.
The echoes dance on twilight's breath,
Awakening dreams, beyond our death.

With shadows deep, the mind takes flight,
To realms of peace, devoid of light.
In solitude, the spirit sings,
Of all that was, and what love brings.

Each whisper soft, a tender call,
A gentle nudge, we may not fall.
The silence wraps us in its grace,
A sacred space, where hearts embrace.

In stillness found, the world can bloom,
Awakening life, dispelling gloom.
Together we rise, as dreams ignite,
In evocations, we find our light.

Reflections of Distant Melodies

In twilight's glow, a tune remains,
A haunting note that softly strains.
Across the hills, the echoes sigh,
A symphony of reasons why.

With every breath, a memory flows,
Of laughter shared and joy that glows.
The strings of time, they weave and bind,
Reflections sweet, of days gone by.

Beneath the stars, the music swells,
In whispered tales, a moment dwells.
Resonating in the evening's kiss,
A serenade, an endless bliss.

Through every note, the heart can soar,
A journey vast, forevermore.
In distant melodies, we find,
The echoes of our souls entwined.

Tears as Unplayed Notes

In silence, shadows weep alone,
Fingers trace the strings of fate.
Each droplet sings a sorrowed tone,
A melody that won't abate.

Unplayed notes float in the dark,
Lost in echoes of the past.
Hope flickers like a tiny spark,
A fleeting moment, fading fast.

Yet in the pain, there's beauty found,
A canvas soaked in shades of gray.
With every tear, new ground's unbound,
Transforming night to break of day.

In the end, they intertwine,
Tears and music, both divine.

The Timelessness of Stillness

In quietude, the world takes pause,
Time suspends its endless race.
Every breath, a gentle cause,
In stillness, we find our grace.

The whispers of the earth emerge,
As nature holds its breath so tight.
In this calm, our souls converge,
A harmony of purest light.

Moments stretch like soft, thin threads,
Binding us to what we feel.
In silence, every heartword spreads,
An unbroken, timeless reel.

Here in stillness, we are free,
Floating in eternity.

Essence of a Whisper

A whisper weaves through the air,
Soft as dawn on sleeping dew.
It dances lightly without care,
Painting dreams in sky so blue.

Secrets shared in muted tones,
Words that flutter, shy and fleet.
In the quiet, hearts atone,
Two souls finding rhythmic beat.

The essence of a wordless pact,
Stronger than the loudest shout.
In silence, feelings get enshrined,
Connection grows without a doubt.

Each whisper holds a world inside,
A treasure that cannot divide.

Notes in the Void

In the stillness, notes dissolve,
Drifting softly through the night.
Each sound a question to resolve,
Chasing echoes, seeking light.

Frequencies of love and loss,
Rest upon the weightless air.
A melody, like gentle toss,
Of starlit dreams, beyond compare.

Voids can sing without a sound,
In space, where silence finds its song.
Each heartbeat, a rhythm profound,
In emptiness, we still belong.

Notes in the void, we embrace,
Finding beauty in empty space.

Tones of Tranquil Yearning

In the whispering breeze, I find peace,
Where ripples of calm gently cease.
Stars shimmering, a soft embrace,
Yearning for time, at a measured pace.

Moonlight serenades the quiet night,
Bathed in silver, a tranquil sight.
Dreams unfold in a gentle sway,
Embracing hopes that softly play.

In the stillness, wishes float free,
Echoes of love, a sacred decree.
Each moment lingers, sweet and pure,
A heart's longing, a timeless allure.

Awake with the dawn, yet still I sigh,
Carried by thoughts that drift and fly.
In the tapestry of night, I roam,
In tones of yearning, I find my home.

Serenade of Stillness

A hush that blankets the world tonight,
In shadows deep, the absence of light.
Gentle whispers dance in the air,
Each breath a moment, a silent prayer.

Moonbeams flicker on tranquil sea,
In the stillness, I long to be free.
Notes of silence weave through my mind,
In this serenade, peace I find.

Crickets sing in the darkened glade,
A melody soft, a calm cascade.
Life slows down in the night's embrace,
Wrapped in stillness, I find my place.

Breath by breath, the world fades away,
In this serenade, I wish to stay.
With dreams that flutter on feathered wings,
In the quiet, my spirit sings.

Lullabies of Lingering Hopes

As twilight falls, the stars ignite,
Whispers of dreams in the velvet night.
Hopes like petals, softly unfurl,
In the cradle of evening, a precious twirl.

Lullabies weave through the dusky air,
Carried on breezes without a care.
Each note a promise, tender and true,
In hearts that whisper, "I'll wait for you."

Moments drift like clouds in the sky,
Painting the canvas as dreams pass by.
Lingering thoughts, a soft caress,
In lullabies found, I find my rest.

Awake with purpose, yet wrapped in peace,
Yearning for dreams that never cease.
In the twilight's glow, hope gently glides,
Along the river where longing abides.

Cadence of Cloaked Desires

In shadows deep, secrets reside,
Whispers of yearnings we tend to hide.
A rhythm pulses, silent yet loud,
In the cadence of love, beneath the shroud.

Hearts entwined in a dance of fate,
Moments shared, yet we hesitate.
Behind closed doors, desires collide,
In the stillness, our dreams abide.

Murmurs of passion, cloaked from view,
In hidden corners, where feelings brew.
Each stolen glance, a spark that ignites,
In the cadence of night, our soul takes flight.

With breath held close, the world fades away,
In the hush of twilight, we long to stay.
Cloaked desires paint the night sky,
As whispers of love begin to fly.

Heartstrings in Hushed Harmony

In twilight's gentle embrace, they sway,
Whispers of love in soft array.
The stars align in a silent dance,
Where shadows play and hearts enhance.

Fingers trace the faded lines,
Moments stolen, love defines.
Each heartbeat sings a tender tune,
Beneath the gaze of the watching moon.

In secret corners, feelings bloom,
Breathless silence fills the room.
Two souls blend in a quiet song,
As night unfolds, they both belong.

Bound in rhythms, lost in time,
Echoes of laughter, sweet as rhyme.
Their silent vows, a binding thread,
In hushed harmony, love is spread.

Notes of a Softened Heart

Tender whispers float on air,
Each note a promise, sweet and rare.
Gentle touch like softest rain,
Melodies that ease the pain.

With every chord, the past retreats,
In the quiet, love repeats.
Chasing shadows, light appears,
Filling silence, calming fears.

A canvas painted with pure grace,
In every silence, a warm embrace.
Harmony lingers, deep inside,
Where softened hearts forever bide.

Strings that bind, yet set us free,
In hidden notes, we find the key.
With every heartbeat softly sung,
A symphony of love begun.

Echoes of Unvoiced Dreams

Beneath the surface, wishes lie,
Hushed desires that never die.
In every glance, a word unspent,
Silent longings, hearts' consent.

The moonlight speaks without a sound,
In shadows, hidden hopes are found.
Gentle breezes carry sighs,
A world of thoughts beneath the skies.

Language of feelings, soft and light,
Guiding us through the endless night.
Timid paths where bravely tread,
In whispered dreams, our hearts are led.

Unspoken truths, like stars, ignite,
Illuminating the darkest night.
Echoes linger in quiet streams,
Feeding the fire of unvoiced dreams.

Resonance of Hidden Sorrows

In corners dim, shadows conspire,
Whispers of grief, a quiet fire.
Memories drown in silent tears,
Hopes entwined with all our fears.

Each heartbeat carries a weight unseen,
In the depths where we've all been.
A song of loss, a haunting strain,
In the quiet, echoes remain.

Time weaves stories of joy and pain,
In gentle rhythms, hearts complain.
Resonance of battles fought,
In every tear, a lesson taught.

Yet in the sorrow, strength can grow,
From hidden depths, resilience flows.
And as the night begins to clear,
The heart finds peace amidst the fear.

Elysian Whispers of the Mind

In realms where soft dreams dance and play,
Thoughts like whispers blossom and sway.
A garden of wonders, lush and bright,
Illuminated softly by starlit night.

Echoes of laughter, of joy and delight,
Fading like mist in the morning light.
Moments captured in fragile frames,
Forever cherished, they sing our names.

Waves of intention, floating on air,
Secrets of the heart laid open and bare.
Each sigh a testament, each breath a sign,
In the tranquil embrace where souls entwine.

In sacred silence, the spirit finds peace,
Through whispers of wisdom, the burdens cease.
Elysian realms where the mind can soar,
In twilight's embrace, forever more.

A Tapestry of Sighs and Shadows

Threads of twilight weave through the night,
Each sigh a shadow, a flickering light.
In the quiet corners where dreams do dwell,
A tapestry woven, a delicate spell.

Whispers of longing drift soft and low,
Capturing moments in the ebb and flow.
Fragments of memories, both joy and pain,
Stitched with the laughter, embroidered with rain.

Through the fabric of time, stories unfold,
In patterns of courage, both timid and bold.
Each heart is a loom, each thought a thread,
In the dance of existence where all are led.

In the stillness, reflections arise,
A canvas of echoes, of truths in disguise.
Sighs of the ancients, of what has passed by,
In shadows we wander, beneath the vast sky.

Quiet Preludes of Reflection

Amidst the stillness, a moment in time,
Quiet preludes rise, soft and sublime.
Thoughts drift like leaves on a gentle stream,
Bathed in the glow of a whispered dream.

The heart finds solace in silence profound,
In the hush of the world, new truths are found.
Fragments of wisdom float softly like mist,
In the tender embrace of the mind's gentle twist.

Each pause a journey, each breath a song,
In the quietude, we finally belong.
A dance of illumination in shadow and light,
Guiding our spirits through the depths of the night.

In the echoes of peace, the heart learns to see,
In quiet reflections, we find the key.
Unlocking the doors to the soul's deeper quest,
In tranquil surrender, we finally rest.

Silent Echoes of Yesterday

Faint whispers linger in the twilight air,
Silent echoes carry a lover's prayer.
Memories painted in shades of the past,
Fleeting and fragile, yet meant to last.

Through corridors of time, shadows unfold,
Stories of heartbeats and dreams once told.
In the dim light, the remnants reside,
Where laughter and tears have gracefully cried.

A tapestry woven with threads of intent,
In the silence, the heart finds content.
Reflections on windows, on lives intertwined,
In the quiet embrace, the soul is aligned.

Days slip away like the softest of sighs,
Leaving sweet traces beneath painted skies.
In the depths of our hearts, we cherish the glow,
Of silent echoes, forever they flow.

Sonnet of Soft Shadows

In twilight's grasp, the shadows softly play,
They whisper secrets of the day now lost.
A dance of light, where night begins to sway,
Embracing darkness, no matter the cost.

Beneath the moon, the silent echoes chime,
Each breath a promise, held within the still.
The stars above remind us of our time,
As whispers weave through night's enchanting thrill.

With every sigh, the shadows come alive,
They cradle fears, yet spark a glimmer bright.
In dreams, we find the strength to truly thrive,
As soft shadows guide us through the night.

In quietude, our stories intertwine,
The sonnet sings of shadows, yours and mine.

Melodic Murmurs Beneath the Stars

The night unfolds with soft melodic hues,
A tapestry of dreams that gently flow.
The stars above, like diamonds in the blues,
They twinkle secrets only night can know.

Beneath the sky, the world is hushed and still,
Each whisper carries tales of long ago.
The moonlight glimmers on the silver quill,
As shadows pen our stories in a row.

With every breath, we sync to nature's tune,
The murmur of the night wraps 'round our hearts.
A serenade beneath the radiant moon,
Where silence blooms and every moment starts.

In perfect harmony, we find our way,
Melodic murmurs guide us through the gray.

Ballad of Breaths Unspoken

In quiet corners of the heart's domain,
There lies a ballad whispering so low.
The breaths unspoken linger like a stain,
Each sigh a memory, soft as falling snow.

The echoes dance upon the evening breeze,
A song of longing echoing through night.
The silence swells like shadows in the trees,
Where dreams take flight, and hearts ignite.

Each heartbeat tells a story yet untold,
A melody woven with threads of chance.
In the still dark, where secrets dare be bold,
We find the courage in a fleeting glance.

The ballad drifts like petals on the stream,
Breaths unspoken cradle every dream.

Nocturne of Forgotten Dreams

In twilight's embrace, the dreams weave their light,
A nocturne whispers softly to the soul.
Forgotten wishes linger in the night,
Their echoes call, a soft, enchanting toll.

Each shadowed corner hides a story deep,
Of laughter lost and hopes that dared to soar.
In starlit silence, memories gently creep,
They dance like ghosts along the moonlit floor.

With every breath, the past begins to fade,
Yet in the dark, those dreams revive once more.
The nocturne plays a tune that's not afraid,
Reclaiming whispers from the heart's own core.

So let the night unfold its tender scheme,
In the nocturne's arms, we find our dream.

Caress of the Unuttered

In whispers soft, the heart does speak,
A touch so light, yet promises peak.
Words unformed, yet deeply felt,
In shadows where true feelings melt.

The silence blooms like velvet night,
Caressing souls with gentle light.
Unseen moments, tender and pure,
In this embrace, all hearts allure.

Time dances slow on breaths we share,
A language rich, beyond compare.
In every glance, a story spins,
In the realm where love begins.

Caught between the spoken and mute,
In every pause, the answers suit.
The unuttered, a sacred space,
Where love transcends and finds its grace.

Light Twinkles of Hope

Stars ignite in the velvet sky,
Each a twinkle, a hopeful sigh.
In the darkness, dreams take flight,
Guided by the softest light.

Beneath the gloom, a glimmer stirs,
A whispered promise, the heart concurs.
Hope's warm glow, a beacon near,
Shimmering softly, calming fear.

Raindrops dance on the windowpane,
Melody sweet, washing pain.
Every droplet, a chance to rise,
Each reflection, a clearer guise.

Gathered wishes in silent prayer,
They flutter softly on the air.
In the stillness, faith ignites,
Light twinkles, shining through the nights.

Silence Wrapped in Melodies

In the stillness, music hums,
Softly weaving, the heart succumbs.
Notes that linger on the breeze,
Wrapped in silence, their sweet tease.

The echo of a gentle tune,
Carried softly by the moon.
Whispers swirl in twilight's grasp,
In this moment, stillness clasp.

Time stands still as shadows play,
While melodies guide the way.
In hidden depths, a song remains,
Where silence nurtures, love retains.

Each heartbeat drifts in perfect rhyme,
Embraced by peace, transcending time.
Wrapped in echoes, softly spun,
In the dance of two, we are one.

The Crescendo of Quiet Dreams

In twilight's breath, the hush unfolds,
A symphony that gently holds.
Dreams arise like wisps of mist,
In silence found, they twist and twist.

Gentle whispers weave through night,
A tapestry of soft delight.
As dreams crescendo, hearts entwine,
In the quiet, our souls align.

Stars align in cosmic play,
While words remain, faint and gray.
The pulse of hope begins to gleam,
In the stillness, we dare to dream.

With every sigh, the dawn draws near,
Embracing all that once was fear.
The crescendo of what we seek,
In quiet dreams, our spirits speak.

The Rhythm of Unsaid Goodbyes

In whispered words, we part,
Beneath a sky that starts to cry.
Each glance a tether, pulling tight,
In silence lingers, soft goodbye.

The fading light wraps shadows round,
Holding memories, weary and warm.
Promises dance in the stillness found,
As hearts beat slow, a quiet storm.

Paths diverge like rivers flow,
With heavy hearts, we let them drift.
Yet echoes of love softly glow,
In every heart, the precious gift.

Though words remain unspoken, still,
The warmth of longing holds us near.
In the rhythm of what we feel,
Unsaid goodbyes, forever here.

Chiming Echoes of the Soul

In the stillness, echoes ring,
Notes arise from depths unknown.
Chimed laughter, soft as spring,
Resonates in heart's true tone.

Whispers weave through gentle night,
Carried by the moon's soft glow.
Each moment felt, a pure delight,
In melodies that ebb and flow.

The soul's song dances in the air,
A symphony of dreams set free.
In every heartbeat, purest prayer,
Harmony in you and me.

Chiming echoes, sweet and clear,
A reminder, we are whole.
In the music that we hear,
Lies the truth of every soul.

Twilight's Sonnet of Stillness

Twilight falls like a velvet cloak,
Embracing earth in hushed embrace.
With every sigh, the stars awoke,
Lighting paths to a sacred space.

The whispering winds hum a tune,
Crickets join in the nightly song.
While shadows dance 'neath the silver moon,
Time pauses here, where we belong.

Stillness wraps the world so tight,
A gentle hush envelops all.
In this twilight, peace takes flight,
Answering every heart's soft call.

As dreams emerge from the dark climb,
Each breath a verse in nature's script.
Twilight's sonnet, in perfect rhyme,
A symphony of stillness, equipped.

Notes from the Heart's Refuge

In quiet corners, shadows play,
Where secrets linger, softly penned.
Notes of solace find their way,
In heart's refuge, love won't end.

Each letter written, inked with care,
A tapestry of hopes and fears.
Every note, a whispered prayer,
A melody that calms the tears.

Within these walls, our stories weave,
Threads of joy, and moments lost.
In heart's embrace, we learn to believe,
Each note a bridge, no matter the cost.

Voices echo in the still night air,
As we pen our dreams, our deepest musings.
Notes from refuge, tender and rare,
A journey mapped through heart's choosing.

Sonnet of the Unseen

In shadows deep, the whispers dwell,
A world unknown, where echoes swell.
Dreams linger here, in silent grace,
Unseen whispers in a hidden space.

Time dances softly, a fleeting breeze,
With every heartbeat, secrets tease.
Life breathes softly, like a sigh,
In silent realms, where shadows lie.

Mysteries twine in the fabric of night,
Guiding the lost with an unseen light.
Though eyes may wander, hearts will know,
The sacred truths that quietly flow.

So listen close to the unseen song,
In the depths of silence, we all belong.
For in the dark, new paths are drawn,
In the dawning light of the waking dawn.

Sighs as Sonorous As Stars

In the velvet night, stars softly sigh,
Whispers of dreams that float on high.
Each twinkle a tale, a gentle plea,
Echoing secrets of eternity.

Through cosmic winds, their voices weave,
An ancient song that weaves and cleaves.
Shimmering lights, they twirl and dance,
In the vast expanse, they take their chance.

A lullaby kissed by the moonlight's glow,
Guiding the hearts that wander below.
With every gust, a wish takes flight,
In the embrace of the starry night.

Let the skies hear our whispered dreams,
Uniting souls in the starlit beams.
For every sigh is a promise spun,
Beneath the infinite, we are all one.

Requiem for Lost Words

In the quiet ether, words fade away,
Echoes of stories we meant to say.
Fragments of thoughts, now lost in the void,
Leaving the heart, alone and devoid.

Pages once filled with laughter and pain,
Now gather dust, a silent refrain.
In libraries hushed, their voices grow dim,
A requiem sung for the words that brim.

Memories linger in whispers and sighs,
Buried deep where the heart quietly cries.
Each syllable cherished, now fading like mist,
In the depths of silence, too precious to list.

Yet in the stillness, their essence remains,
Woven in dreams, through joy and through rains.
Though lost are the words, their spirit won't fade,
In the hearts of the ones who loved what we made.

Harmony in Muteness

In muted grace, we find our peace,
Where silence reigns, all troubles cease.
Beneath the stillness, a deep refrain,
The heart's soft whispers, a sweet gain.

In empty spaces, beauty blooms,
Quiet moments dispel the glooms.
Harmony hums in the hush of night,
Where echoes gather, soft and light.

Between the notes of a silent song,
We learn to listen, to belong.
In the pause of breath, in the sighs we share,
There's music born from the love we bear.

So cherish the silence, hold it near,
In the depths of quiet, there's nothing to fear.
For in this calm, our souls entwine,
Creating a melody, pure and divine.

The Language of Faint Breaths

In whispers soft, the night reveals,
A tale of stars, the heart conceals.
A sigh of dreams on gentle air,
The language spoken, light as prayer.

Each heartbeat hums, a silent voice,
In shadows deep, we find our choice.
Faint echoes dance, we feel their grace,
A fleeting glance, a warm embrace.

The moonlight glows, a silver thread,
We follow paths where visions tread.
In tender moments, truth emerges,
Through quiet sighs, our hope converges.

With every breath, connections grow,
In whispered tones, our spirits flow.
A tapestry of dreams we weave,
In quiet nights, we dare believe.

Murmurs Beneath the Surface

In still waters, secrets dwell,
Life's soft murmurs, a gentle swell.
Ripples speak of days gone by,
Underneath the azure sky.

A hidden depth, a world unseen,
Where whispers drift, and shadows glean.
Each ripple tells a silent tale,
Of dreams that rise and hopes that sail.

The current runs, a soft caress,
In quiet depths, we find our rest.
Murmurs call, from deep inside,
With every pulse, our souls abide.

The heart listens to nature's song,
In every note, we find where we belong.
Through darkest nights, we seek the light,
Murmurs guide, till dawn ignites.

Serenade of Sundown Shadows

As daylight fades, the shadows play,
In hues of gold, they dance and sway.
A serenade of twilight's grace,
They whisper softly, time can't erase.

The sun bows down, a gentle sigh,
Painting skies where dreams can fly.
Each shadow grows, a story spun,
In evening's glow, all hearts are one.

Beneath the dusk, a calming touch,
Where silence speaks, we see so much.
A lullaby of fading light,
In shadows' arms, we hold the night.

Through every shade, the world transforms,
With twilight's breath, new hope reforms.
In serenades, we find our way,
As shadows turn to night from day.

Tranquil Chords of the Soul

In quietude, the heart can hear,
The tranquil chords that draw us near.
Each note a thread, weaves peace profound,
In gentle waves, our souls are found.

The music swells, a sweet refrain,
In silent spaces, joy and pain.
Harmony nestled within the strife,
The essence of our shared life.

With every chord, connections bloom,
In softest whispers, dispel the gloom.
As melodies embrace the night,
We find our path, a guiding light.

In tranquil tones, we breathe, we sigh,
With every chord, we learn to fly.
In symphonies that gently roll,
We play the song of every soul.

Interlude of Lingering Thoughts

In the quiet corners of my mind,
Memories whisper, gentle yet unkind.
Each moment lingers, a fleeting sigh,
Chasing echoes that never die.

Dreams entwined with the threads of time,
A tapestry woven, in rhythm and rhyme.
Fragments of laughter, shadows of tears,
Carried softly through the years.

Within this space, I find my way,
Through reflections of yesterday.
A heartbeat's echo, a moment's embrace,
Lingering thoughts, a warm trace.

As time drifts on, I pause and choice,
To listen deeply, to hear their voice.
In this interlude, a dance unfolds,
Of stories whispered and secrets told.

Shadows Dancing in Solitude

In the stillness of the evening light,
Shadows flicker, weaving in flight.
Each movement whispers of forgotten lore,
Dancing gently across the floor.

Lonely figures, their secrets kept,
In quiet corners where silence wept.
They twirl and spin, a ghostly embrace,
Cloaked in solitude, lost in grace.

Outside, the world buzzes, alive with sound,
While here, it's the shadows that are unbound.
Their rhythm flows, an unspoken trance,
In the dark, they sway, they dance.

A gallery of phantoms, dressed in dreams,
Caught in moonlight's soft silver beams.
In solitude's arms, they find their song,
A harmony whispered where they belong.

Serene Silence of the Night

Under the blanket of starlit skies,
The world exhales, and softly lies.
Each breath a whisper, a calming wave,
In the serene silence, the heart finds its cave.

Moonbeams drape over tranquil seas,
A gentle hush carried by the breeze.
Stars twinkle secrets in the velvet dome,
Guiding lost souls, calling them home.

In this stillness, thoughts take flight,
Floating softly into the night.
Wrapped in shadows, embracing the dark,
A symphony born from silence's spark.

Here, peace reigns, a glorious sound,
In the depths of night, serenity found.
Each pause, each breath, a lullaby sweet,
In the night's embrace, the heart skips a beat.

The Interval Between Heartbeats

In the quiet pause, a heartbeat holds,
A fleeting moment, as time unfolds.
In the space between, life's whispers cling,
Where silence blooms, and dreams take wing.

Each tick of the clock, a gentle sigh,
Moments trapped as they drift by.
In that interval, the world stands still,
A breath, a thought, a heart to fill.

Through that silence, a truth divine,
Connecting souls like a fragile vine.
In every heartbeat, a spark ignites,
In that sweet stillness, life invites.

So here I dwell, in this sacred space,
Between heartbeats, I find my place.
In whispers soft, where secrets lie,
The interval breathes, a soothing sigh.

Vessel of Tranquil Thoughts

In the quiet of the night,
Thoughts drift softly like a kite.
Floating free on gentle air,
Whispers of dreams lead us there.

Rivers of calm flow through my mind,
In this silence, peace I find.
A vessel made of fragile glass,
Holding moments that shall pass.

Stars above glimmer faintly bright,
Guiding shadows with soft light.
Each reflection, a silent cheer,
Voices of hope, sweet and clear.

Wrapped within this calm embrace,
Thoughts dissolve without a trace.
A journey deep in silent seas,
Navigating with gentle ease.

A Chorus of Fleeting Moments

A melody of laughter played,
In echoes of the joy we've made.
Each note dances, a spark of glee,
Moments stitched in memory.

Time will turn its endless page,
Each heartbeat, a fleeting stage.
In the chorus, we find our song,
In the rhythm, we all belong.

Glistening hours, they slip and flow,
Like raindrops in the morning glow.
Capturing both the sweet and slight,
In the symphony of light.

Every glance, a love in bloom,
Filling up the empty room.
Together we create a sound,
In fleeting moments, joy is found.

Still Waters Reflecting Wishes

Still waters lie in gentle grace,
Reflecting dreams that time can't erase.
A tranquil lake so clear and deep,
Holds secrets that the shadows keep.

Beneath the surface, hopes will glide,
In every ripple, wishes bide.
Carried softly on a breeze,
They float away with perfect ease.

Each moment still, a precious art,
Casting visions like a dart.
Gazing deep into the night,
We find our wishes take to flight.

With every star that graces sky,
A whispered wish begins to sigh.
Still waters hold what hearts conceal,
In quietude, our dreams reveal.

Musing in the Absence of Sound

In stillness blooms a vibrant thought,
In absence of echo, we are caught.
Silent musings dance in air,
Tranquil moments shared with care.

Time stretches thin as shadows play,
A canvas vast, where thoughts can sway.
Each silence speaks, profound and wide,
In these halls, reflections bide.

The world outside fades far away,
In gentle quiet, here we stay.
Thoughts unfold like petals sweet,
In the calm, our souls retreat.

Listen closely to the hush,
In its depths, a sacred rush.
Musing in this endless ground,
Finding peace in the soundless round.

Reverie in a Quiet Corner

In shadows where the whispers play,
A gentle breeze guides thoughts away.
Petals dance on a silken stream,
Carrying the weight of a wistful dream.

Sunlight filters through the leaves,
As time slows down, the spirit weaves.
A symphony of silence unfolds,
In quiet corners, the heart beholds.

Soft murmurs of the day's embrace,
In this nook, I find my space.
The world outside fades to gray,
In reverie, I long to stay.

The Art of Stillness

Amidst the chaos, a breath is drawn,
The world holds its breath at dawn.
In stillness lies a hidden grace,
A tranquil heart in a hurried race.

Moments linger, softly they blend,
Like whispers of a cherished friend.
With every pause, the soul takes flight,
Finding peace in the gentle night.

In silence, thoughts begin to bloom,
Casting away the shadows of gloom.
The art of stillness, quietly speaks,
As the spirit soars, the heart seeks.

Cadence of the Heart's Yearning

A gentle throb beneath the skin,
In every heartbeat, where love has been.
Whispers echo through the night,
In the cadence, dreams take flight.

Fleeting moments, soft and sweet,
Like distant waves upon the feet.
Each sigh a note in love's refrain,
In yearning, hope and joy remain.

The pulse of life, a tender call,
In every rise, in every fall.
Cadence echoes through the dark,
Igniting once more love's spark.

Unseen Songs of Solitude

In solitude, the heart can sing,
To the rhythm of the quiet spring.
Notes unspoken fill the air,
In unseen songs that linger there.

The silence wraps like a soft embrace,
Revealing truths in empty space.
With each soft breath, a story spun,
Of battles fought and victories won.

A melody found in the gentle night,
In moments steeped in soft twilight.
Unseen songs echo through the soul,
In solitude, we become whole.

Lyrics of Yearning in Twilight

In the dusk of fading light,
Dreams take flight beyond the night.
Whispers linger on the breeze,
Heartfelt sighs among the trees.

Stars awaken, softly gleam,
Guiding us in a shared dream.
Time stands still, while shadows play,
Yearning hearts lead us astray.

Hope ignites beneath the veil,
Love's sweet song begins to tale.
Through the twilight's gentle grace,
We find peace in this embrace.

Melodies of Unspoken Echoes

Silence speaks in whispers low,
Echos dance where feelings grow.
Between the lines, a tune unfolds,
Hidden truths that remain untold.

A glance shared, a fleeting sigh,
Melodies in the boundless sky.
Lost in thoughts that softly wane,
Yearning lingers, sweet yet pain.

Through the shadows, sounds entwine,
In quiet depths, our souls align.
Each heartbeat plays a timeless score,
As dreams linger, forevermore.

Whispered Cadence in the Night

Stars breathe softly in the dark,
While secrets flicker, leaving marks.
Moonbeams weave a tender thread,
Connecting hearts where hopes are fed.

In the stillness, shadows grow,
A symphony of soft aglow.
Each whispered note a sweet refrain,
Hushing doubt, inviting gain.

Through the night, we walk as one,
In whispered cadence, love begun.
With every step, a pulse alive,
In this rhythm, we will thrive.

Lament of Quietude

In tranquil moments, shadows weep,
Reflecting dreams we wish to keep.
A quiet sigh beneath the stars,
Lamenting of our hidden scars.

The world outside begins to fade,
A sanctuary where hearts parade.
In solitude, we find our space,
An echoing void we must embrace.

Yet in silence, solace lies,
Boundless hopes beneath the skies.
Lament may linger, but so will light,
Guiding us through the darkest night.

Reflection in the Quiet Room

Soft whispers dance around the walls,
Where shadows play and silence calls.
Thoughts drift gently, like autumn leaves,
In the stillness, the heart believes.

Golden sunbeams pierce the night,
Casting dreams in soft, warm light.
Memories linger, like a gentle tune,
In this haven, where dreams commune.

Time slows down, a tender grace,
Each moment here, a sacred space.
The world outside fades far away,
In the quiet room, I long to stay.

Reflections dance upon the floor,
A symphony of thoughts galore.
With each breath, the spirit sings,
In the calm, the soul takes wings.

Harmonies Beneath the Surface

Ripples shimmer on the lake,
A melody in each small break.
Secrets whisper in the breeze,
Carried softly through the trees.

Beneath the waves, a world unseen,
Where shadows play and colors gleam.
In every depth, a story flows,
In hushed tones, the spirit knows.

Harmony sings in underwater light,
A dance of joy, a pure delight.
In the currents, life's song swells,
With every heartbeat, magic dwells.

Listen closely, hear the sound,
A symphony of life unbound.
Beneath the surface, love's embrace,
In shadows deep, we find our place.

The Unwritten Word

Blank pages wait for thoughts to bloom,
In the silence rests potential's room.
Every stroke a chance to see,
The stories locked inside of me.

Words unspoken, dreams untold,
In the heart, they shimmer gold.
Each blank line, a world to weave,
In letters' dance, we dare believe.

Ink flows slowly, like a stream,
Crafting visions, chasing dreams.
With every phrase, a truth emerges,
In written thoughts, the soul converges.

The unwritten whispers to the brave,
Inviting hearts, daring to save.
Embrace the silence, let it guide,
For in the void, our dreams reside.

A Memorable Echo

In the valley, sounds return,
Carried softly, hearts will yearn.
A call from deep, the mountains reply,
In the stillness, voices sigh.

Memories bounce against the stone,
Reminding us we're not alone.
Each echo holds a piece of time,
In whispers sweet, in rhythm and rhyme.

Through every valley, every rise,
The past lingers, never dies.
In the music of the air,
A reminder of love, a timeless prayer.

A memorable echo, let it soar,
A reminder of what came before.
In every heartbeat, every pulse,
The echoes linger, and life convulse.

Milton Keynes UK
Ingram Content Group UK Ltd.
UKHW030750121124
451094UK00013B/796

9 789916 908174